MW01349198

BEAR FAIRY EDUCATION

Tracing Letters & Numbers, Early Learning Workbook, Ages 3 4 5

© 2018 BEAR FAIRY EDUCATION. All rights reserved.

No part of this book may be reproduced in any written, electronic, recording, or photocopying form without written permission of the author.

Published by: BEAR FAIRY EDUCATION.
Interior Design by: Pani Palmer, Kentucky
Cover Design by: Pani Palmer, Kentucky

10 9 8 7 6 5 4 3 2 1
1. Workbook for Kids 2. Basic Early Learning Children Book
First Edition

a a a a a a a a

A A A A A A A A

A is for
anteater

B
is for
beaver

B B B B B B B B

a a a a a a a a

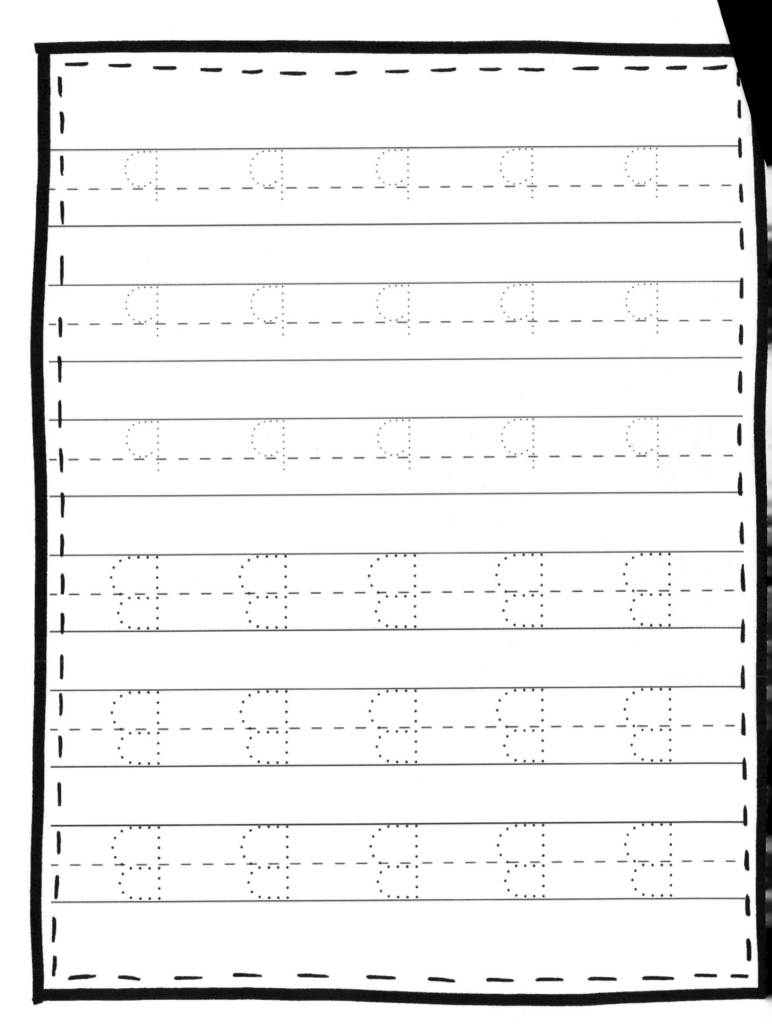

e e e e e e e e e e

E

E is for elephant

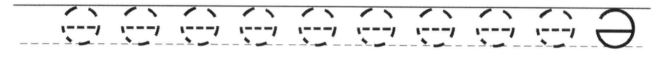

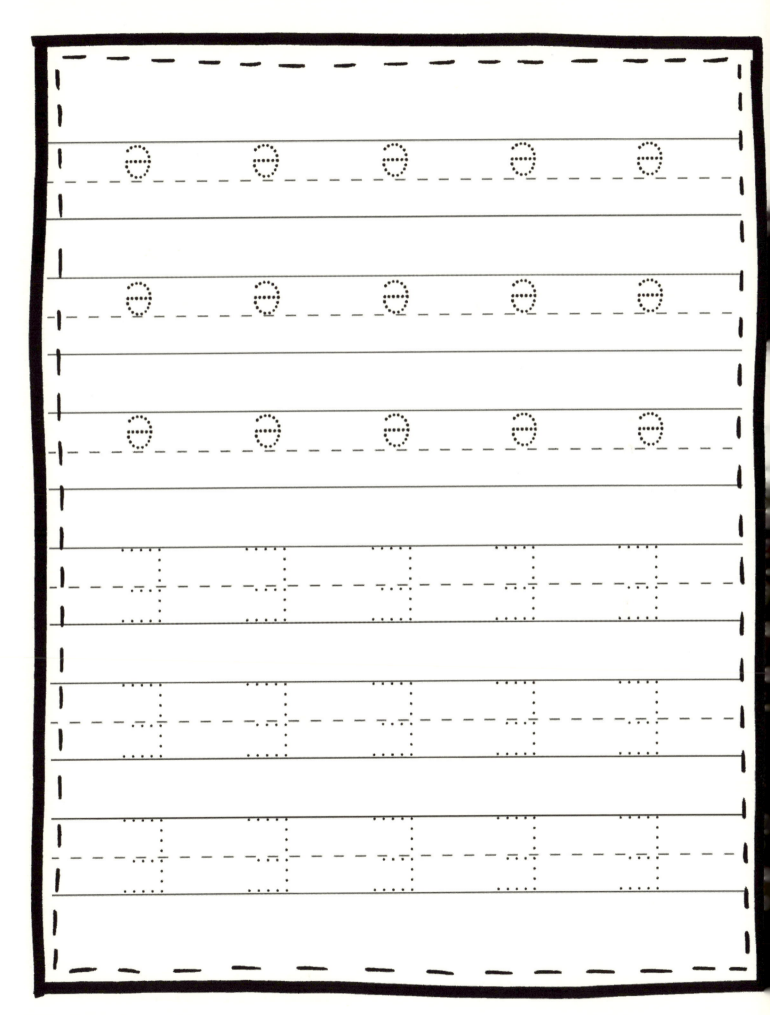

f f f f f f f f f f

F F F F F F F F F

F is for frog

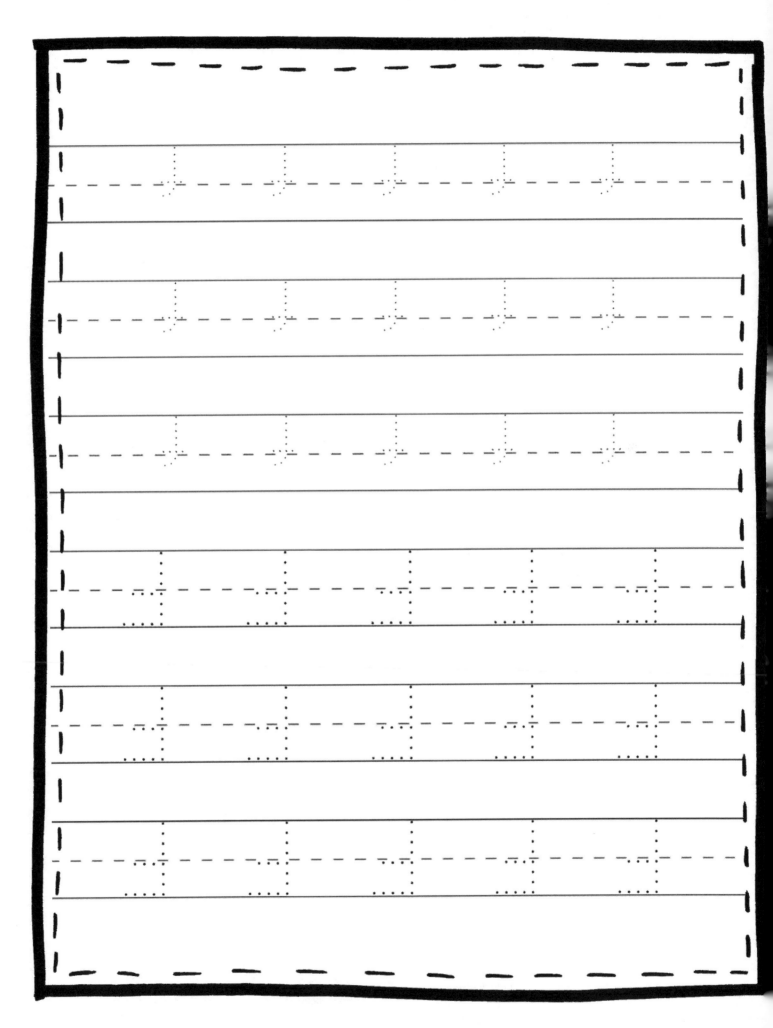

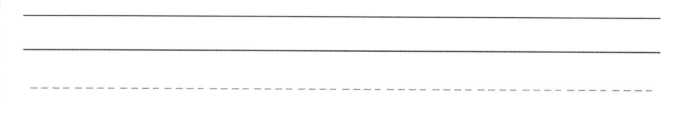

G is for
gorilla

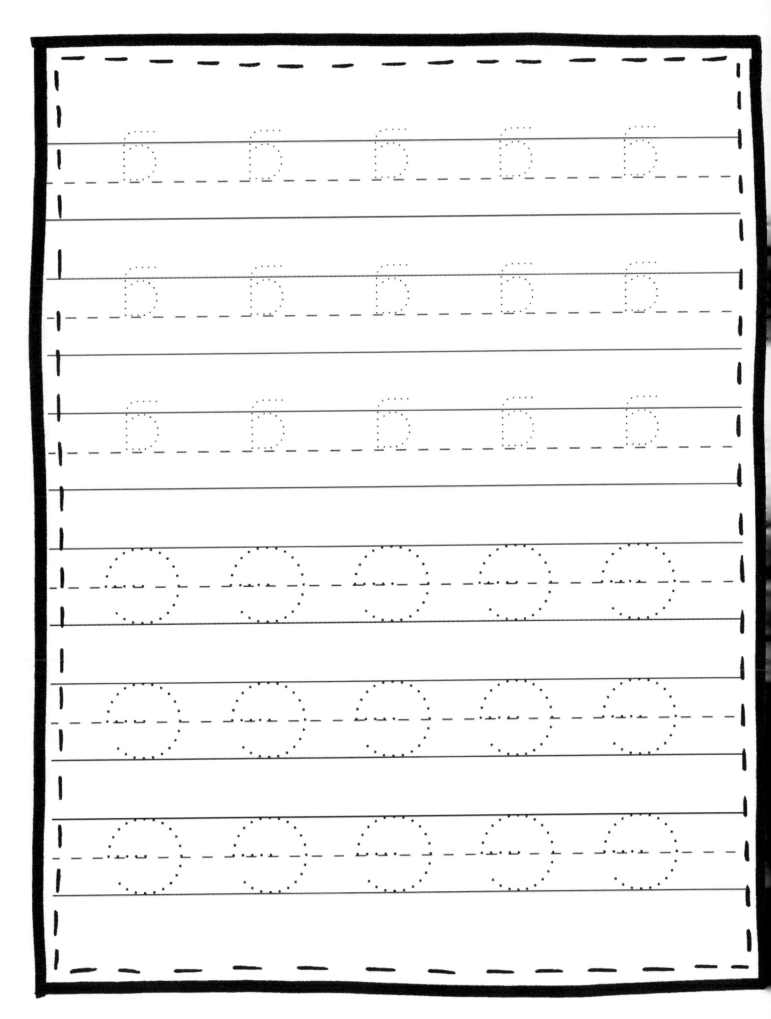

H is for
hippo

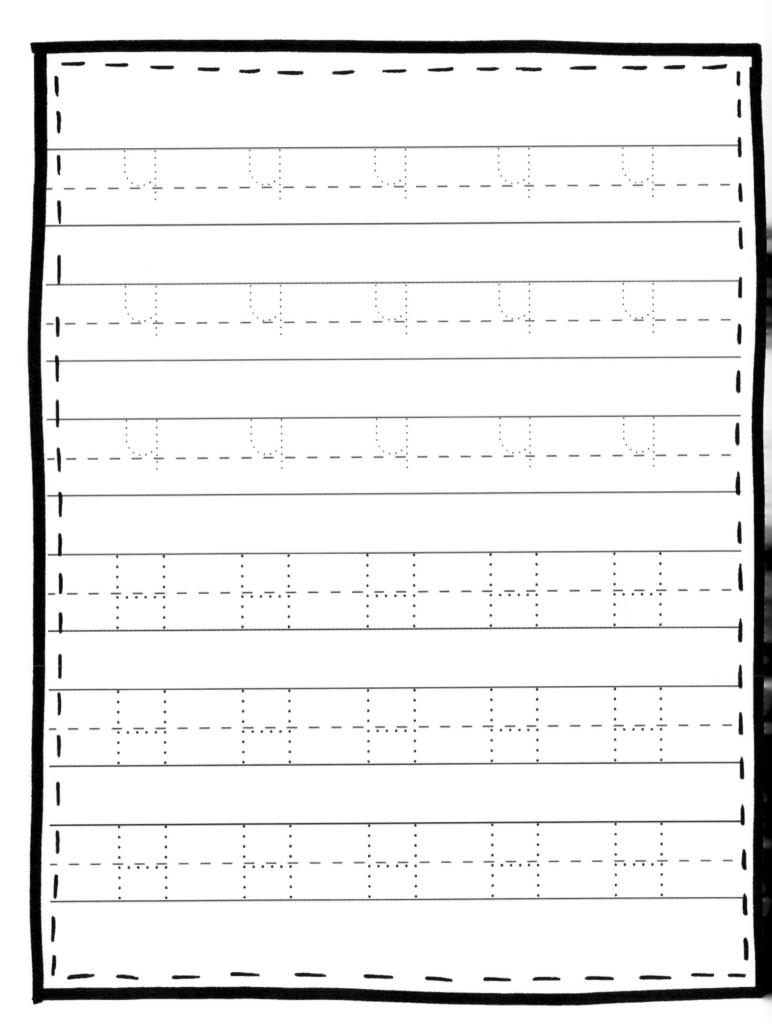

i i i i i i i i i

I I I I I I I I

I is for
iguana

jjjjjjjj

JJJJJJJJJ

J is for jellyfish

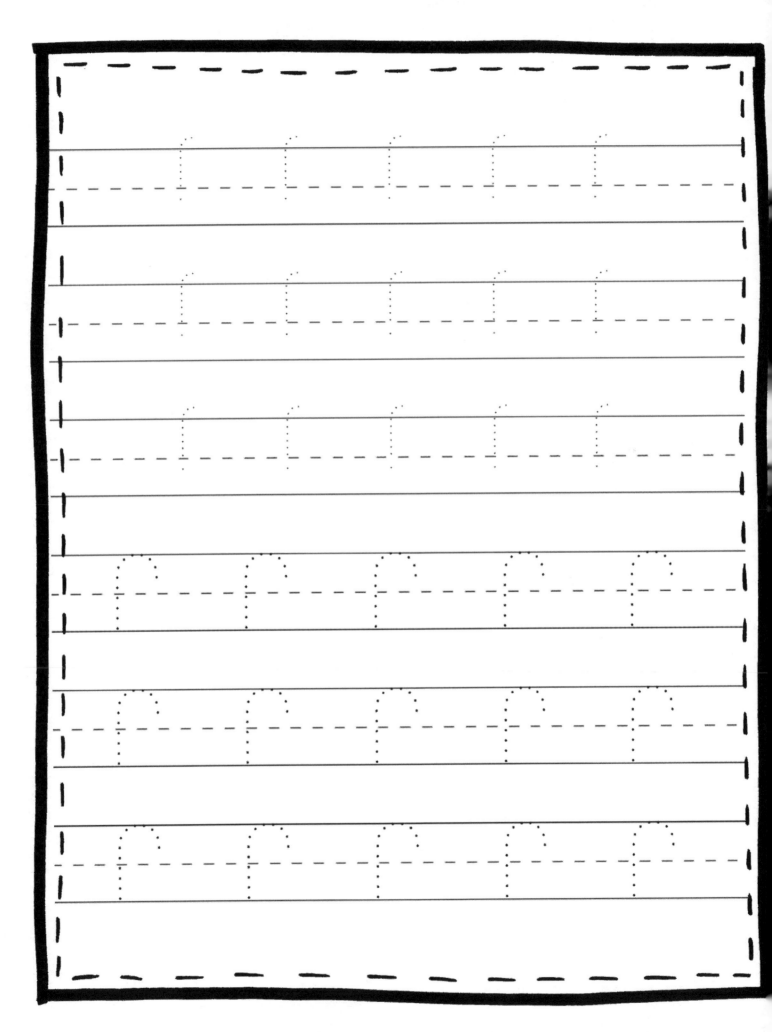

K is for
Kangaroo

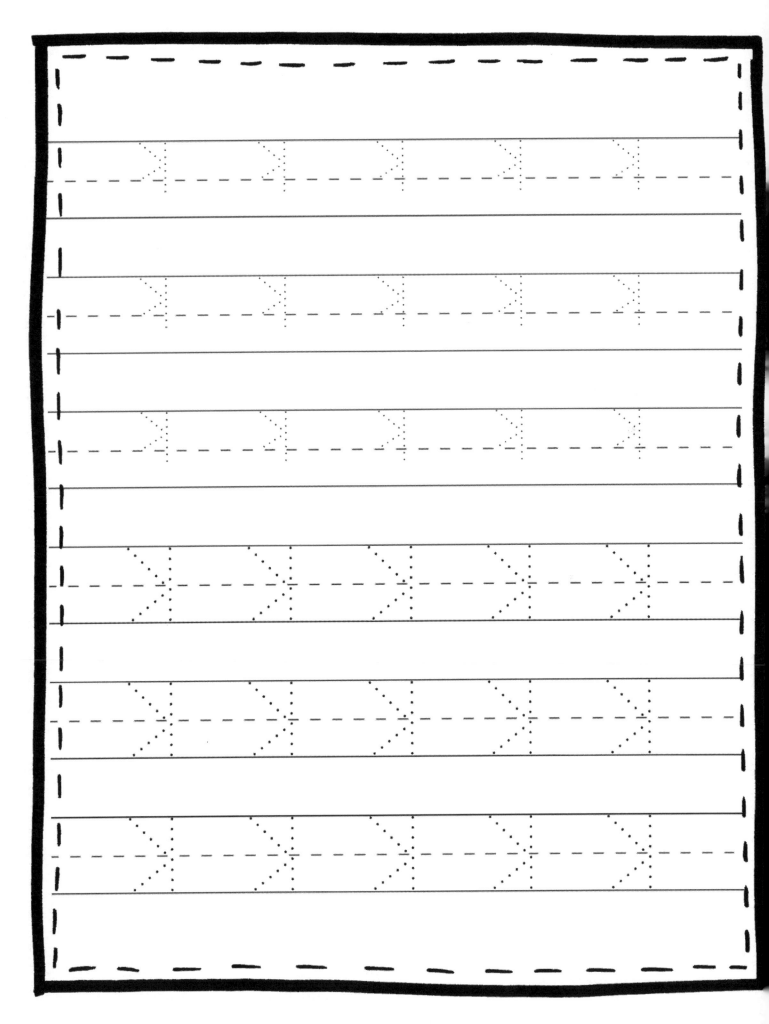

L is for
lion

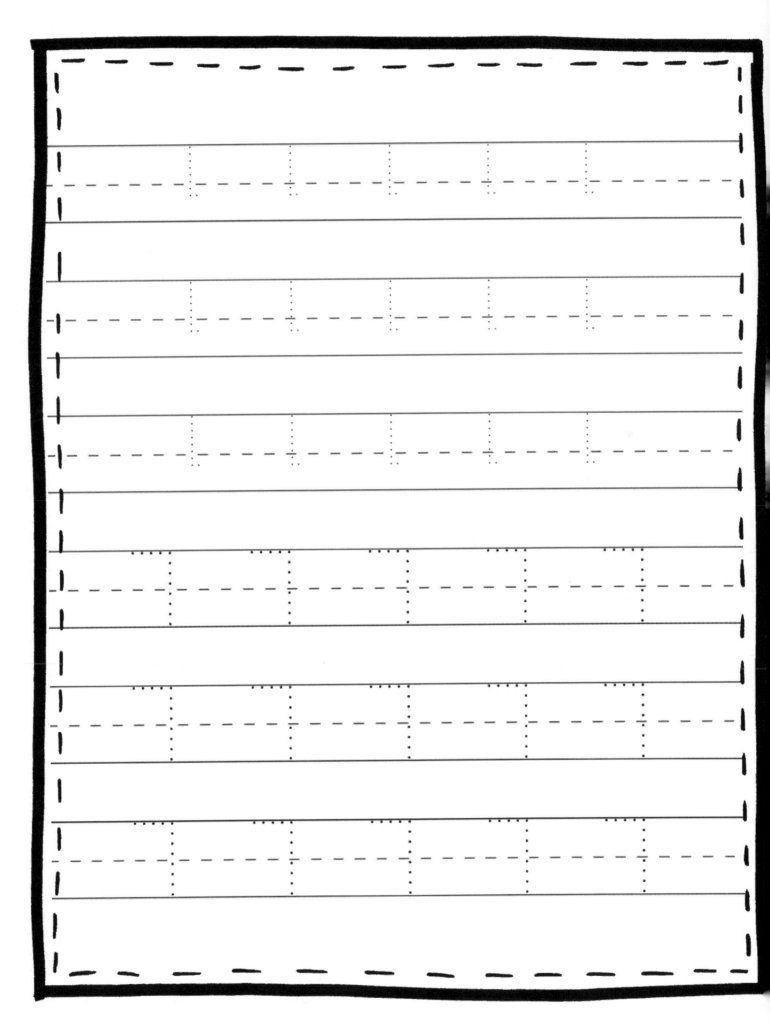

_ _ _ _ _ _ _ _ _ m

_ _ _ _ _ _ _ M

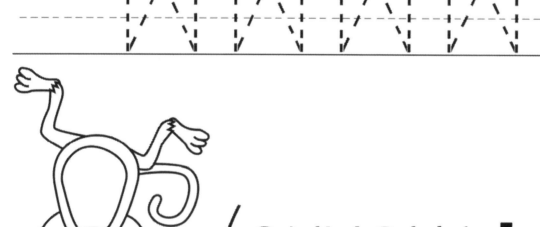

M is for monkey

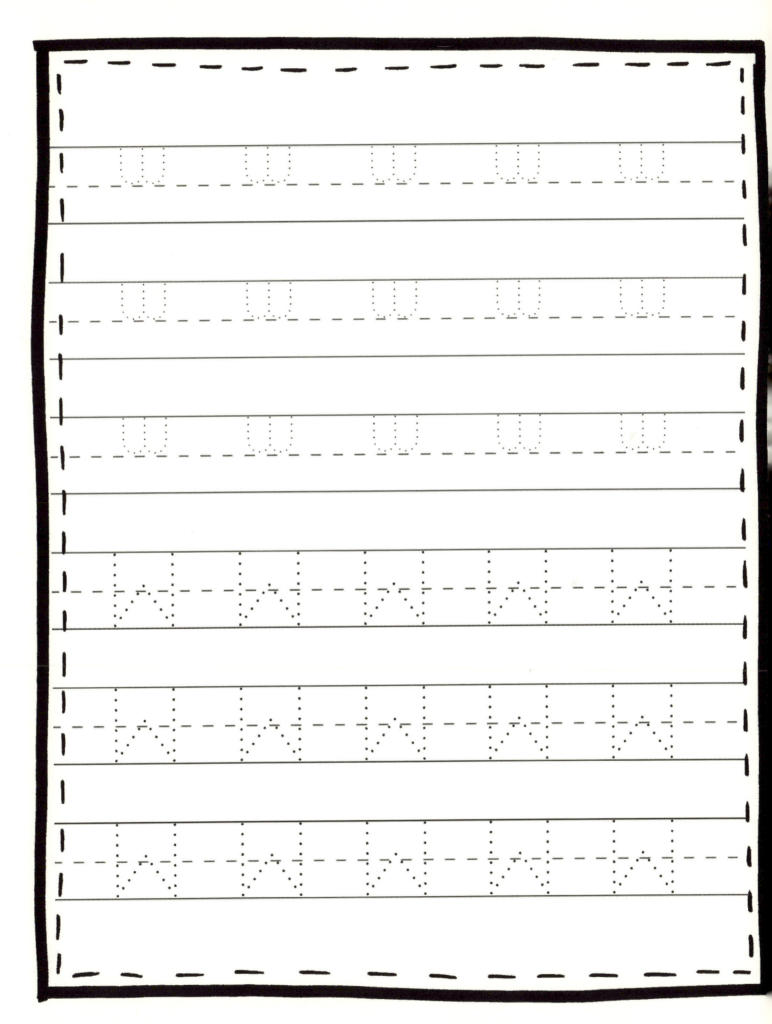

n

N

N is for
narwhal

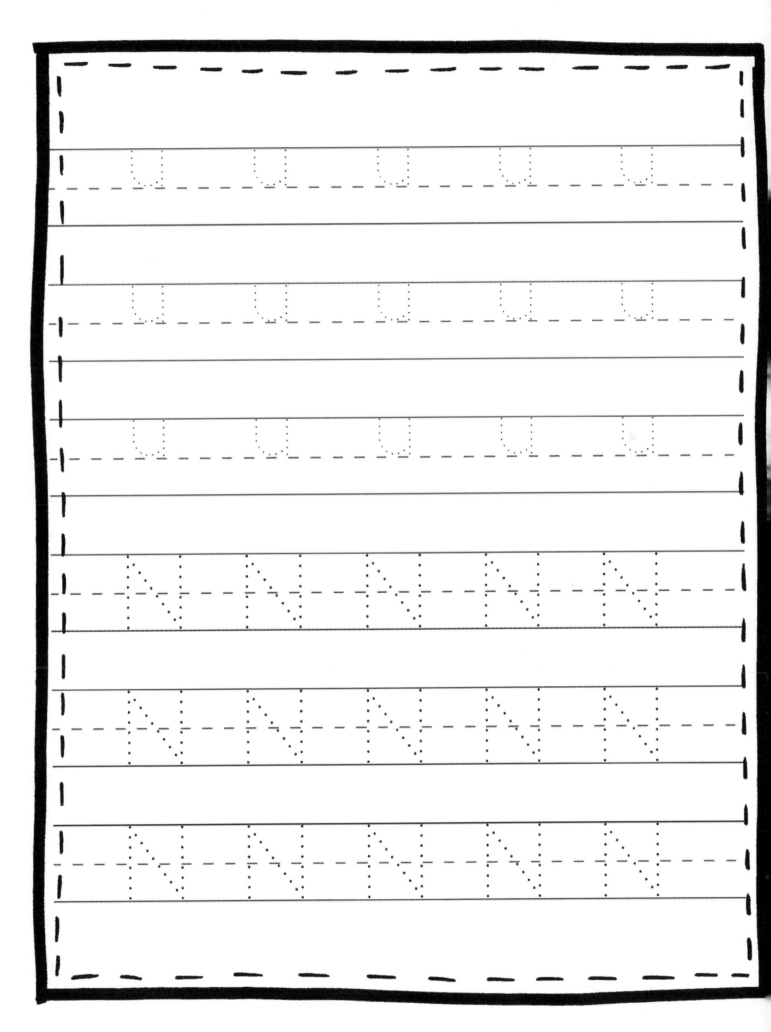

O is for
ostrich

d d d d d d d

D D D D D D D

P is for
panda

P

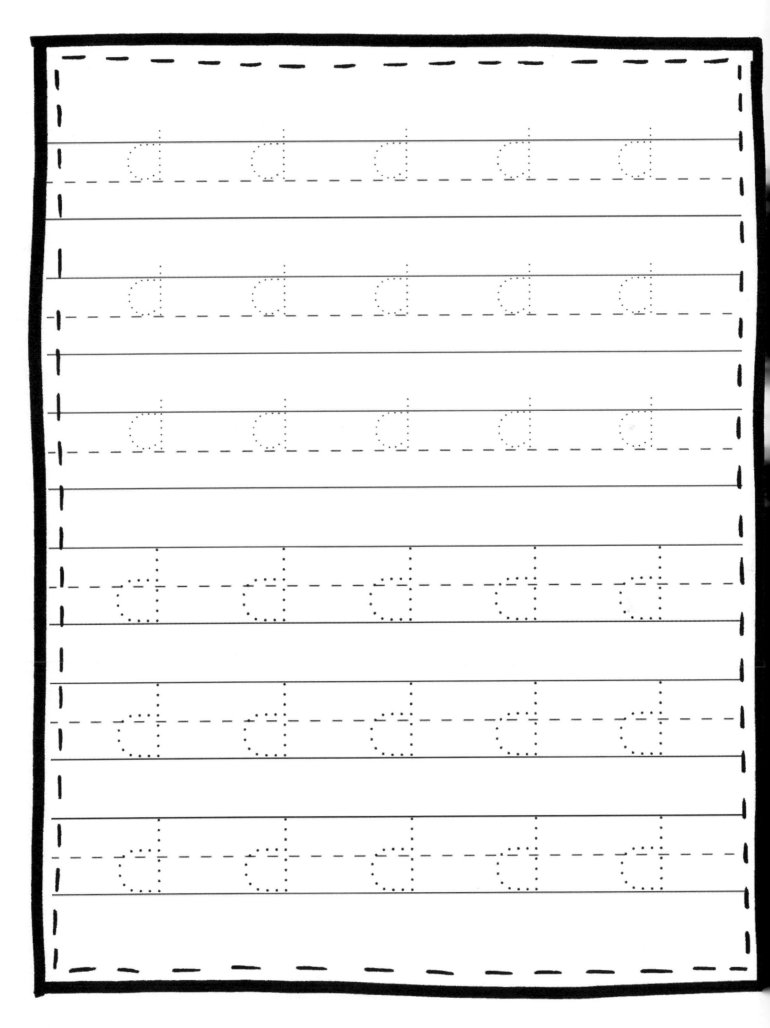

Rr

is for raccoon

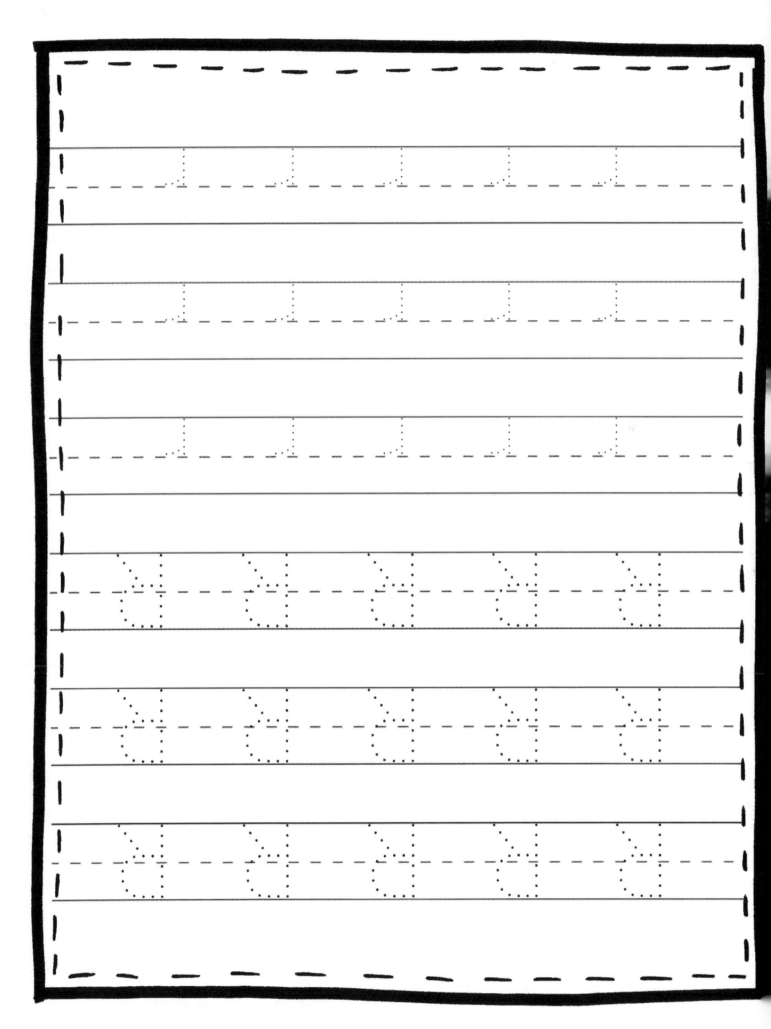

s s s s s s s s s s s

S S S S S S S S

S
is for
snail

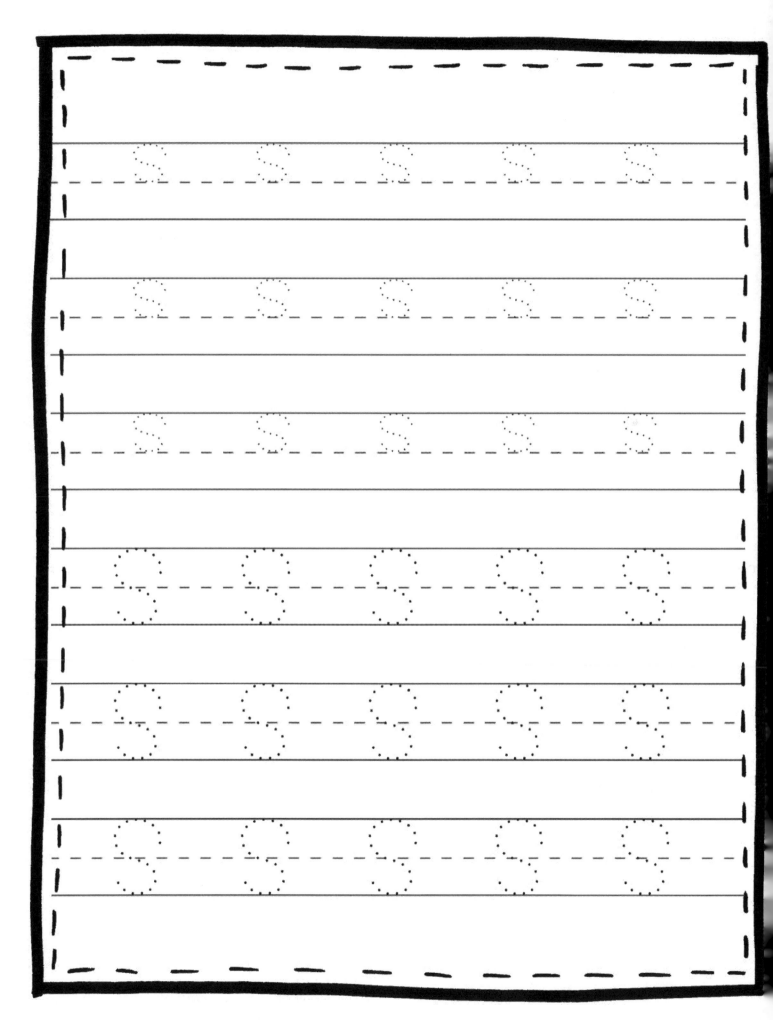

T T T T T T T T T T T T T T

t t t t t t t t t t t t t

T is for tiger

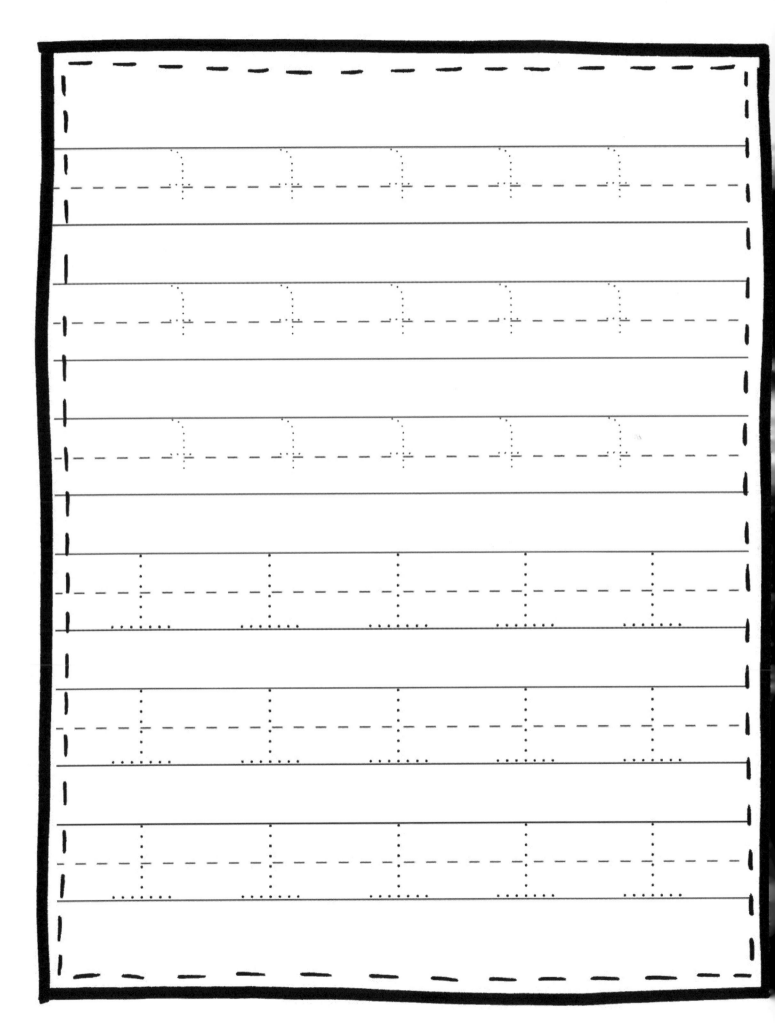

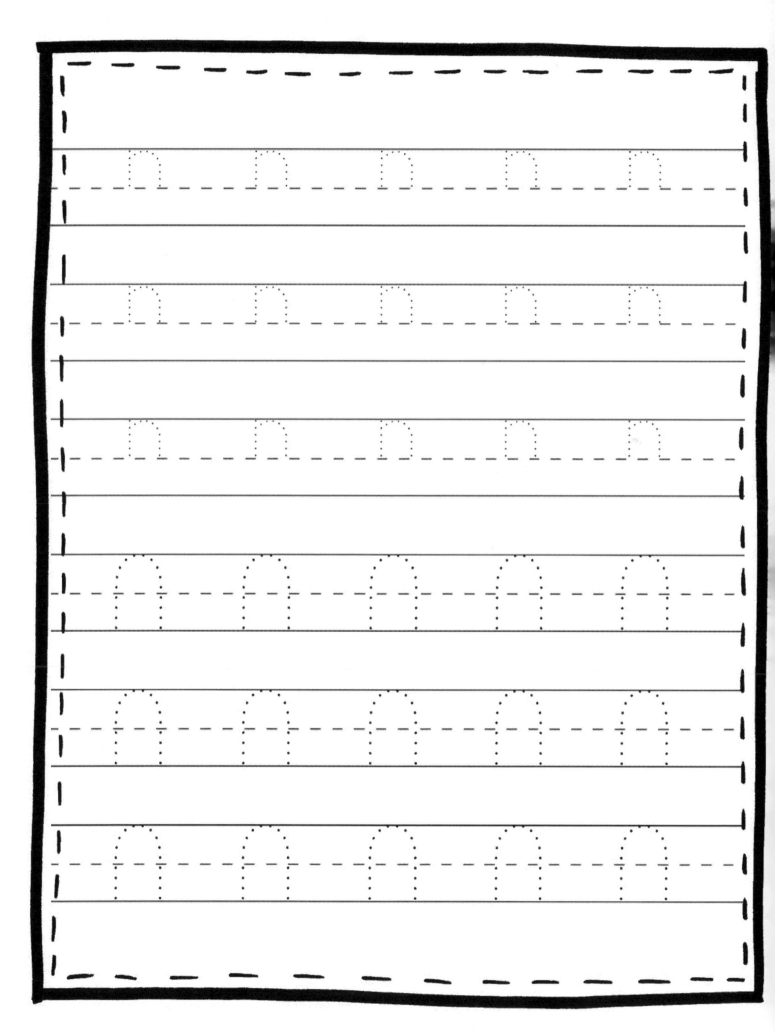

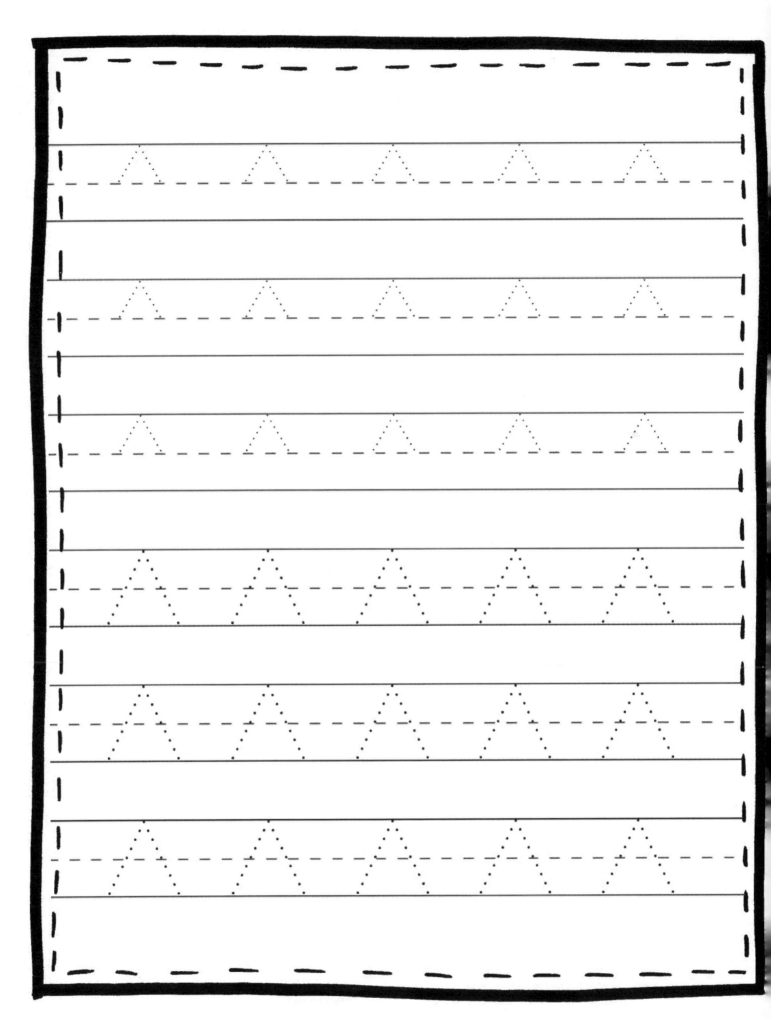

W is for
walrus

| M | M | M | M | M |

| M | M | M | M | M |

| M | M | M | M | M |

| M | M | M | M | M |

| M | M | M | M | M |

| M | M | M | M | M |

X X X X X X X X X X X

x x x x x x x x

X is for
ox

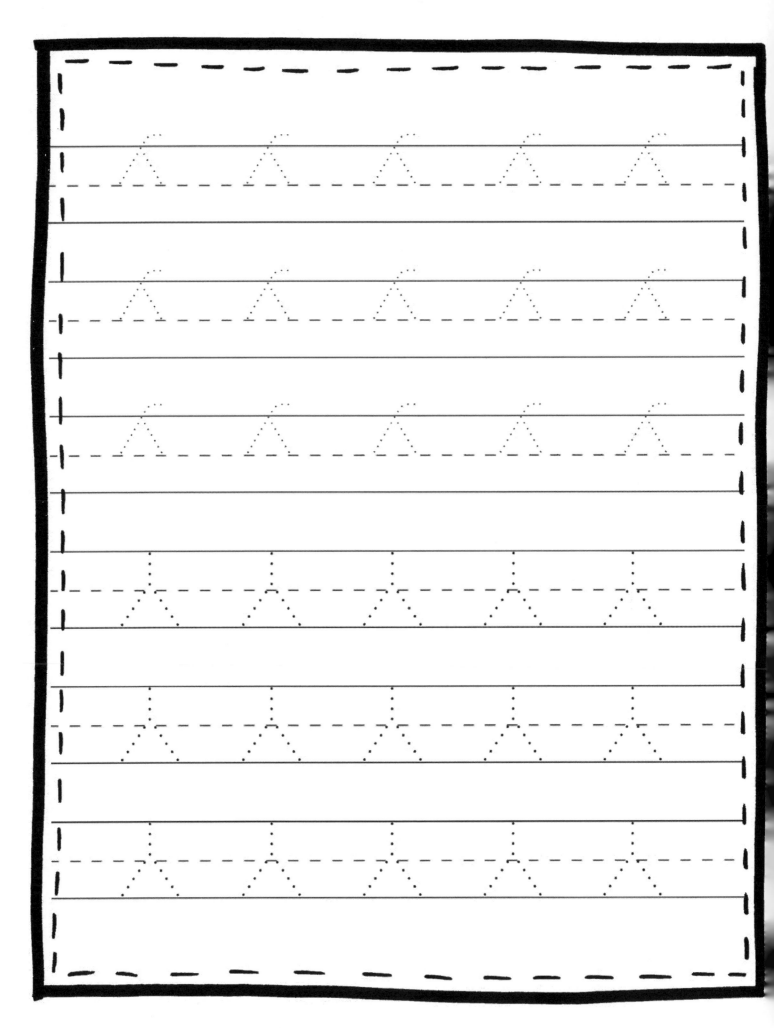

Trace and write the number.

Color the number word.

one

Show the number on the ten frame.

Color 1 star.

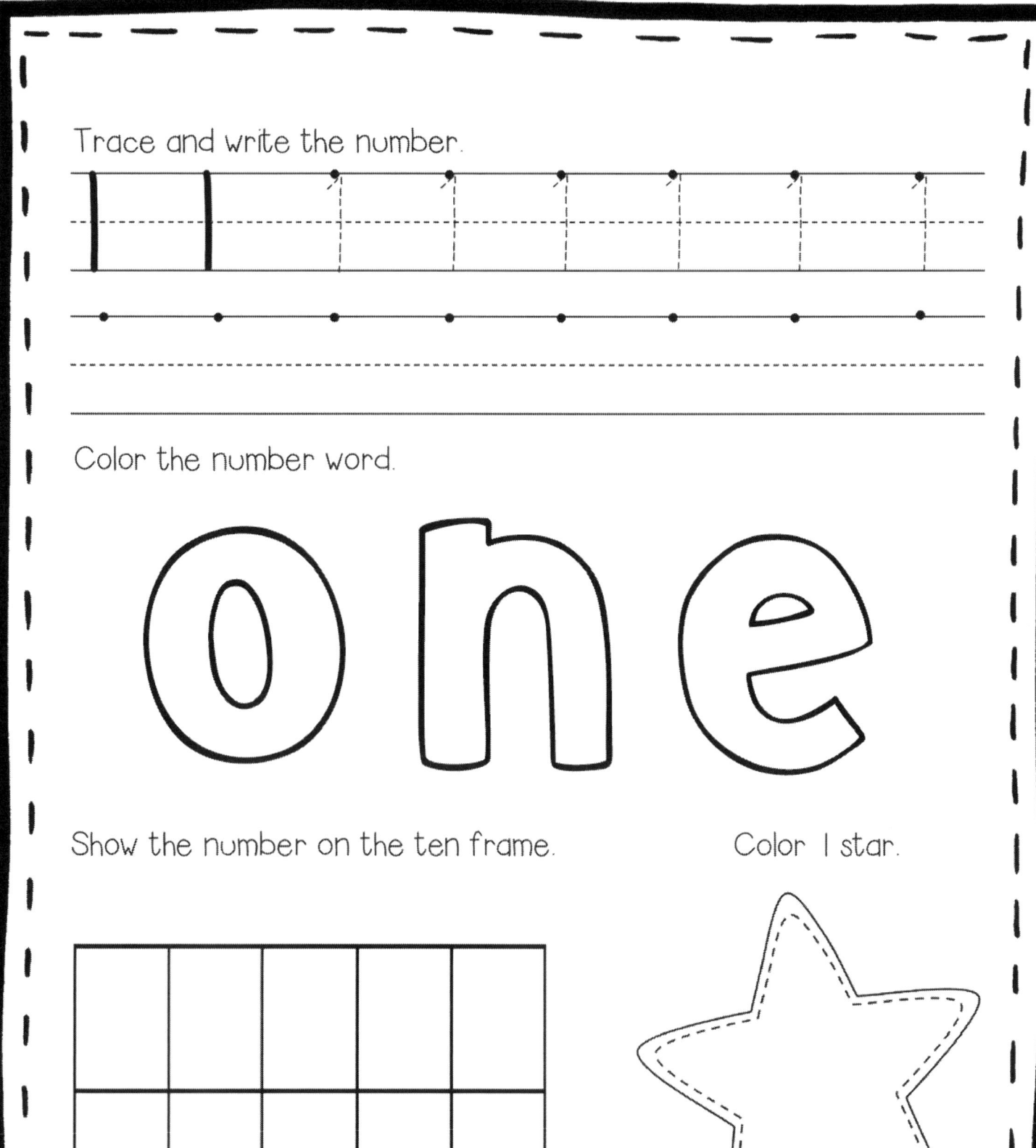

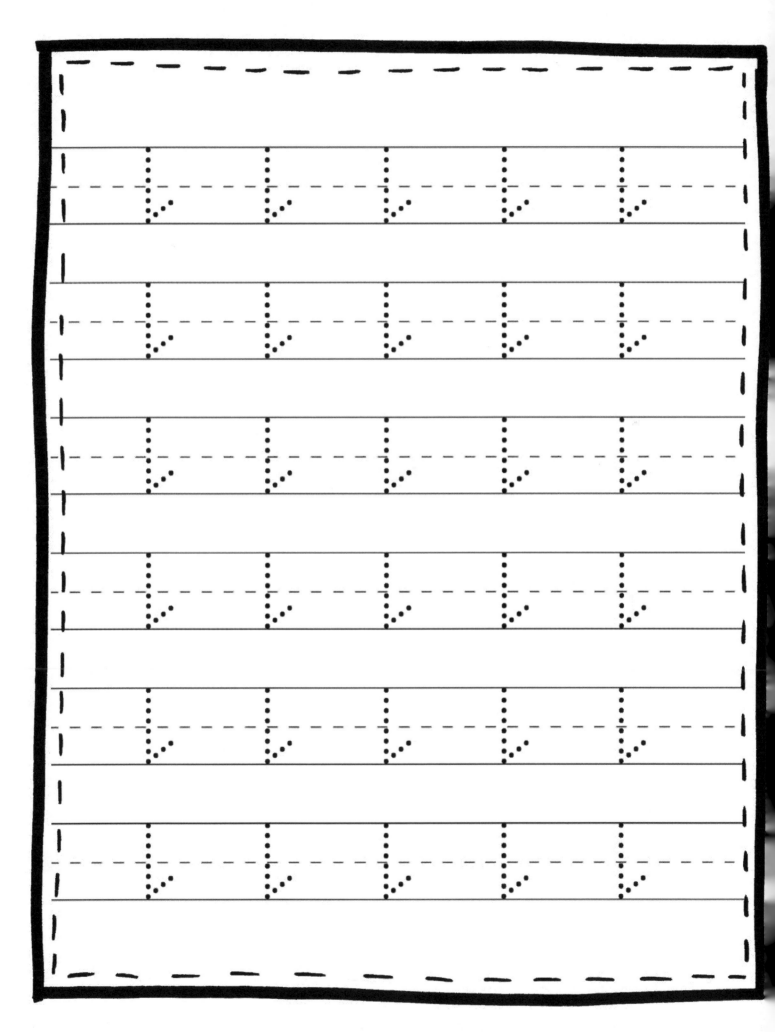

Trace and write the number.

2 2 2 2 2 2 2 2

Color the number word.

two

Show the number on the ten frame.

Color 2 stars.

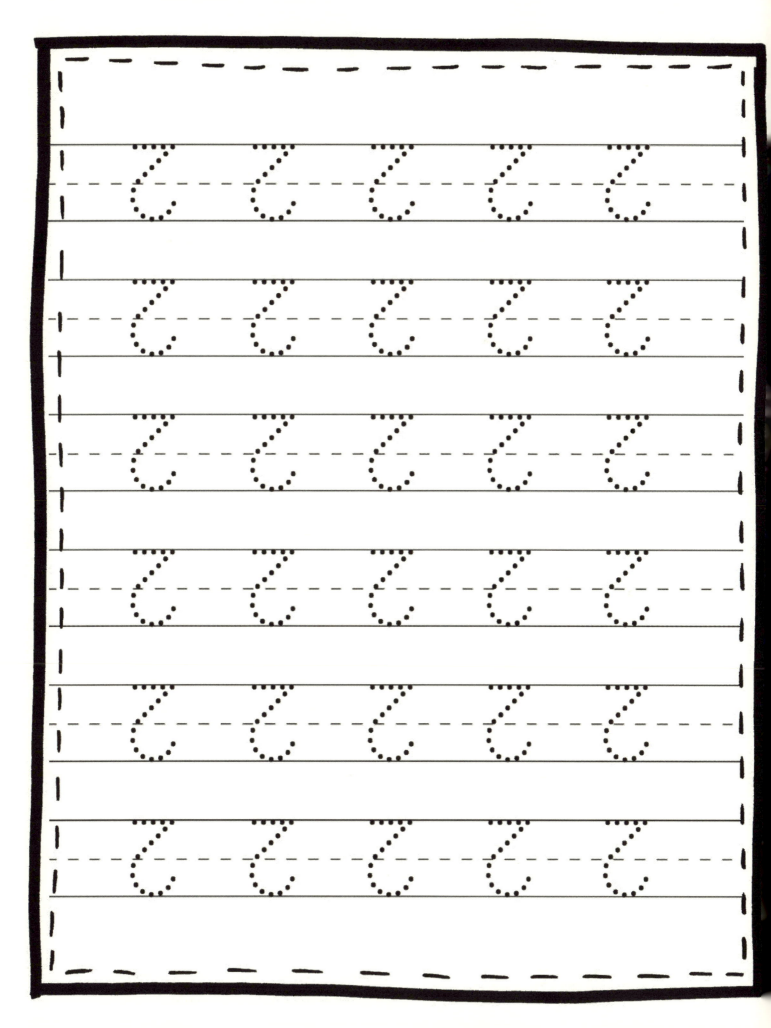

Trace and write the number.

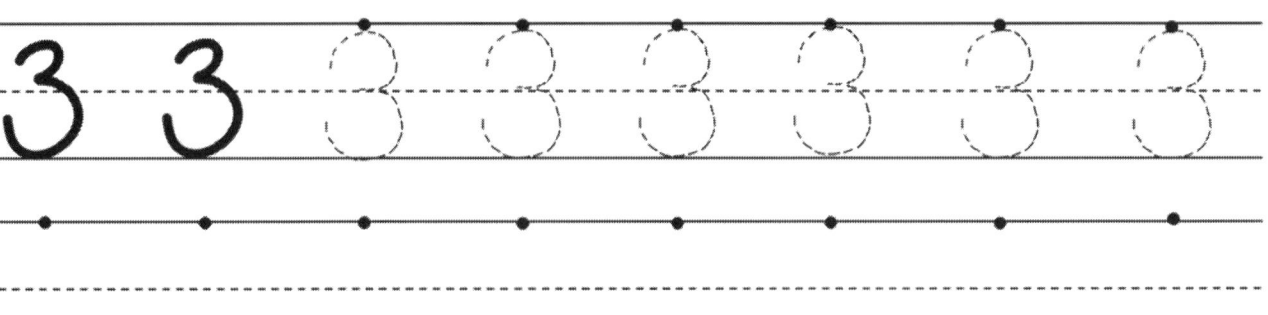

Color the number word.

Show the number on the ten frame.

Color 3 stars.

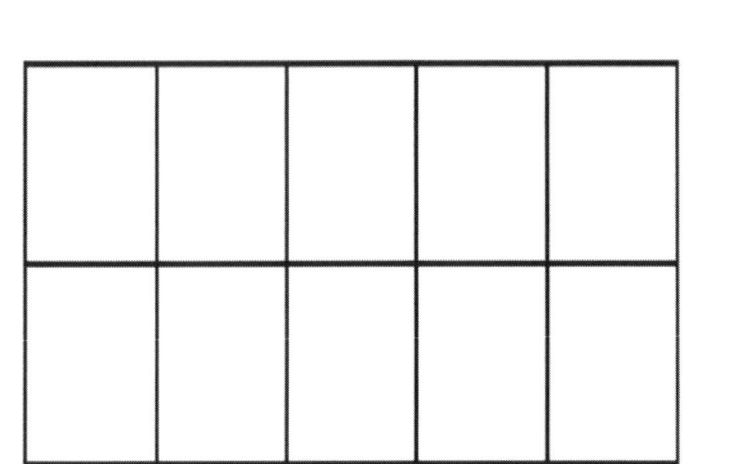

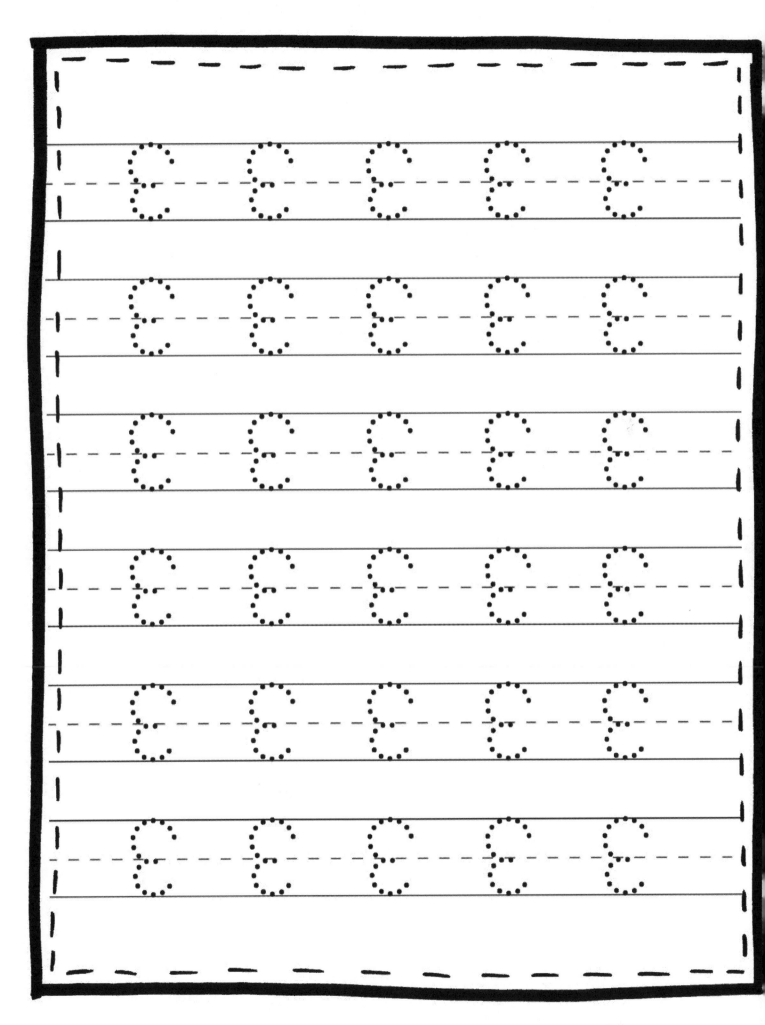

Trace and write the number.

4 4 4 4 4 4 4 4

Color the number word.

four

Show the number on the ten frame.

Color 4 stars.

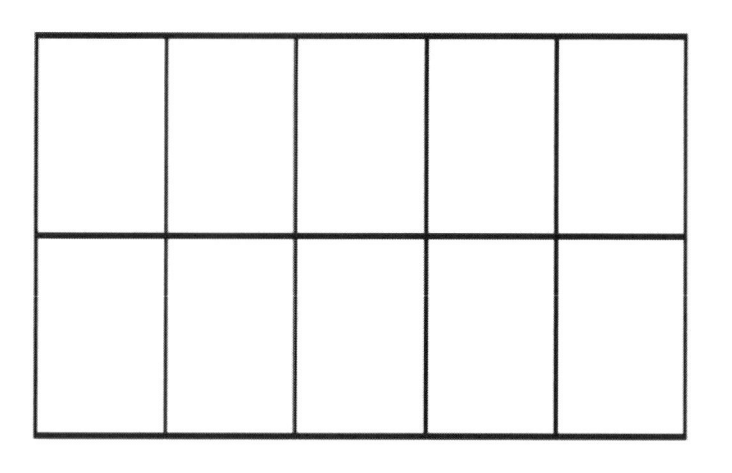

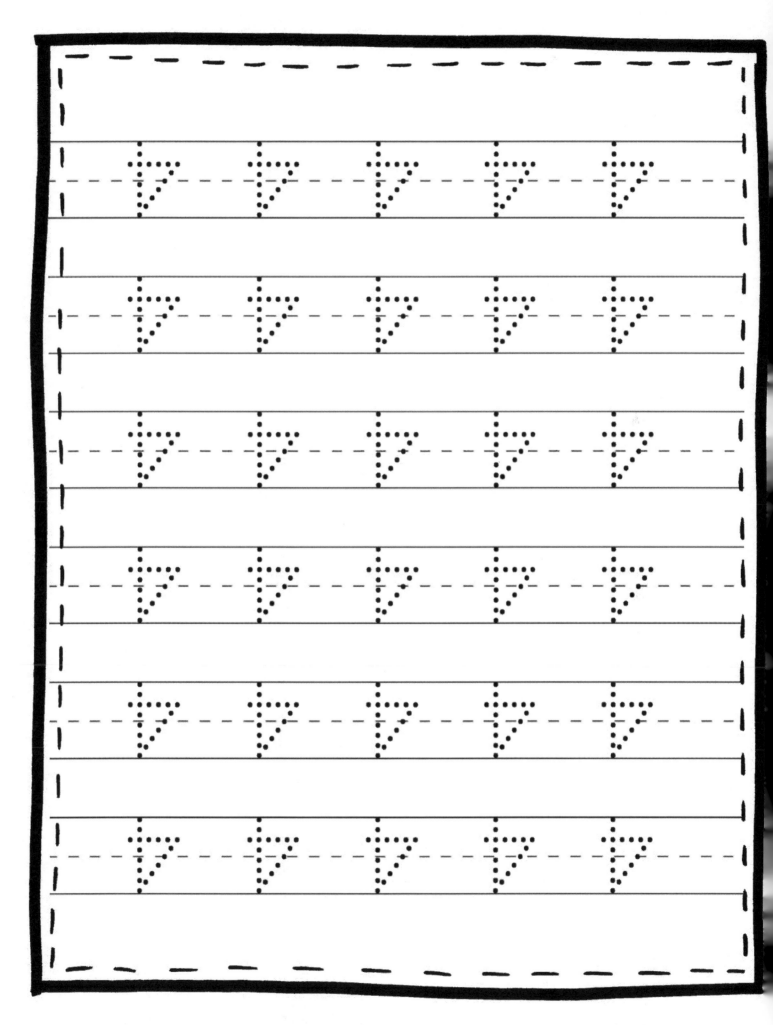

Color 5 stars.

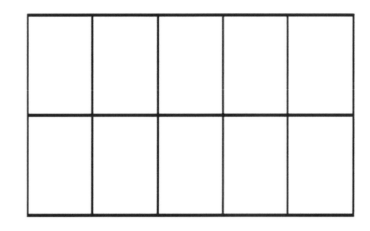

Show the number on the ten frame.

five

Color the number word.

Trace and write the number.

5 5 5 5 5 5 5 5

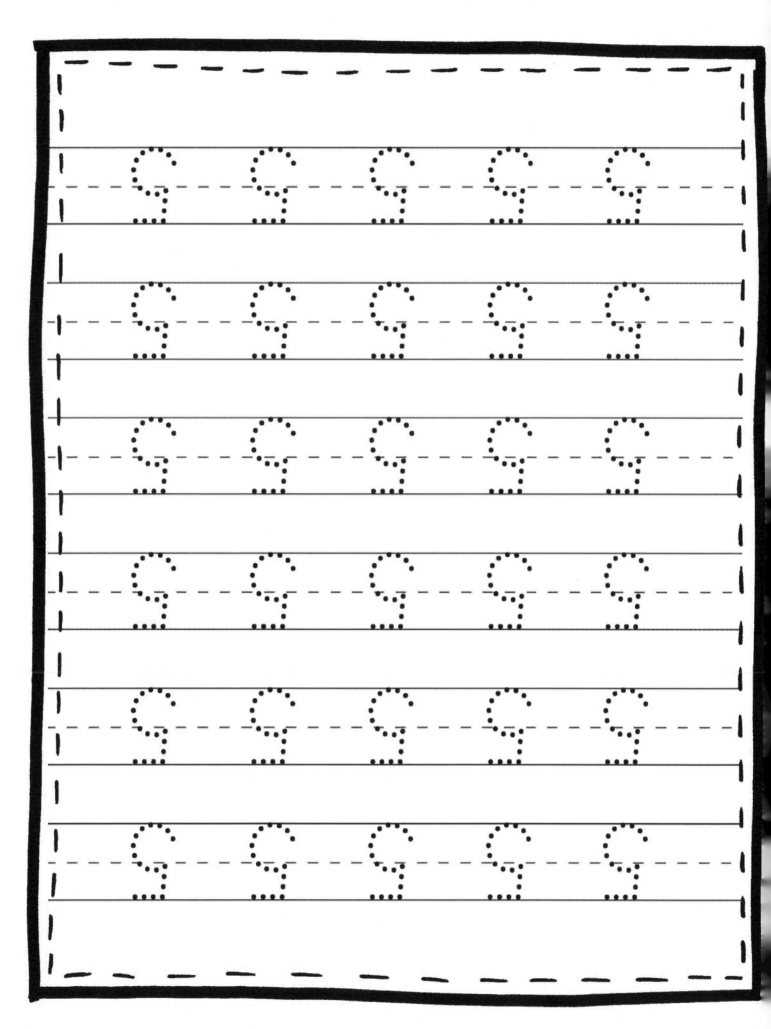

Trace and write the number.

6 6 6 6 6 6 6 6

Color the number word.

six

Show the number on the ten frame.

Color 6 stars.

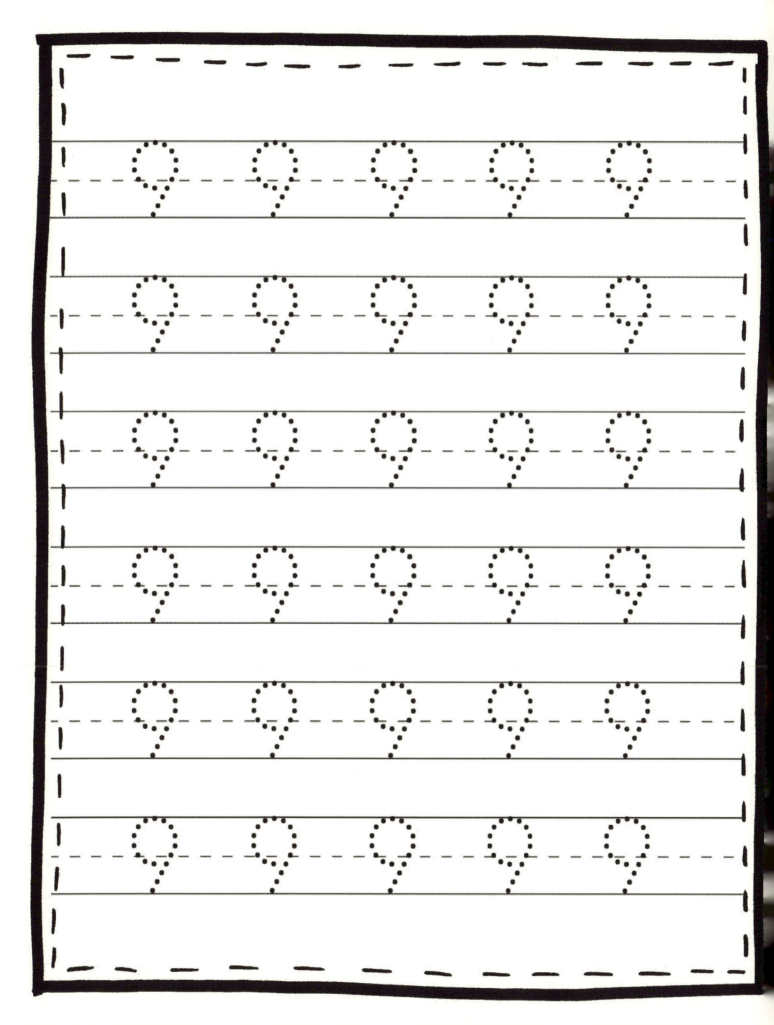

Trace and write the number.

7 7 7 7 7 7 7 7

Color the number word.

seven

Show the number on the ten frame.

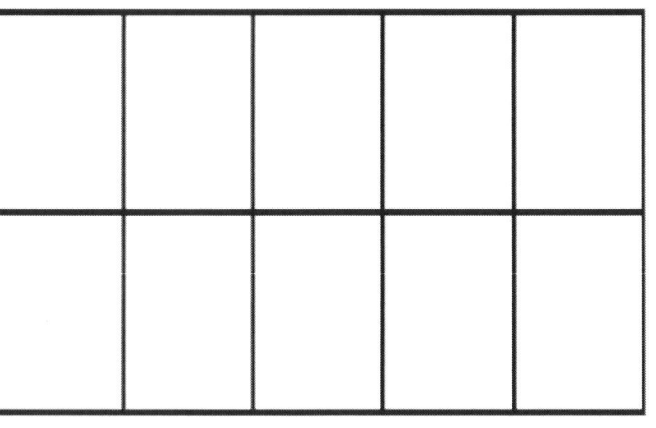

Color 7 stars.

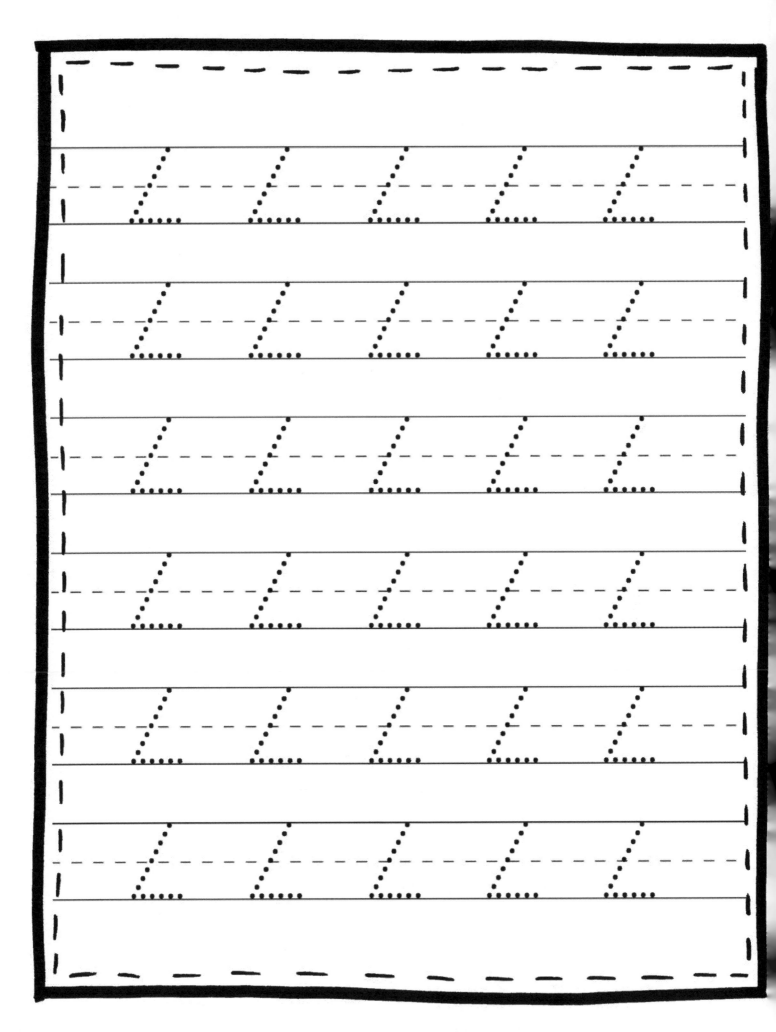

Trace and write the number.

8 8

Color the number word.

eight

Show the number on the ten frame.

Color 8 stars.

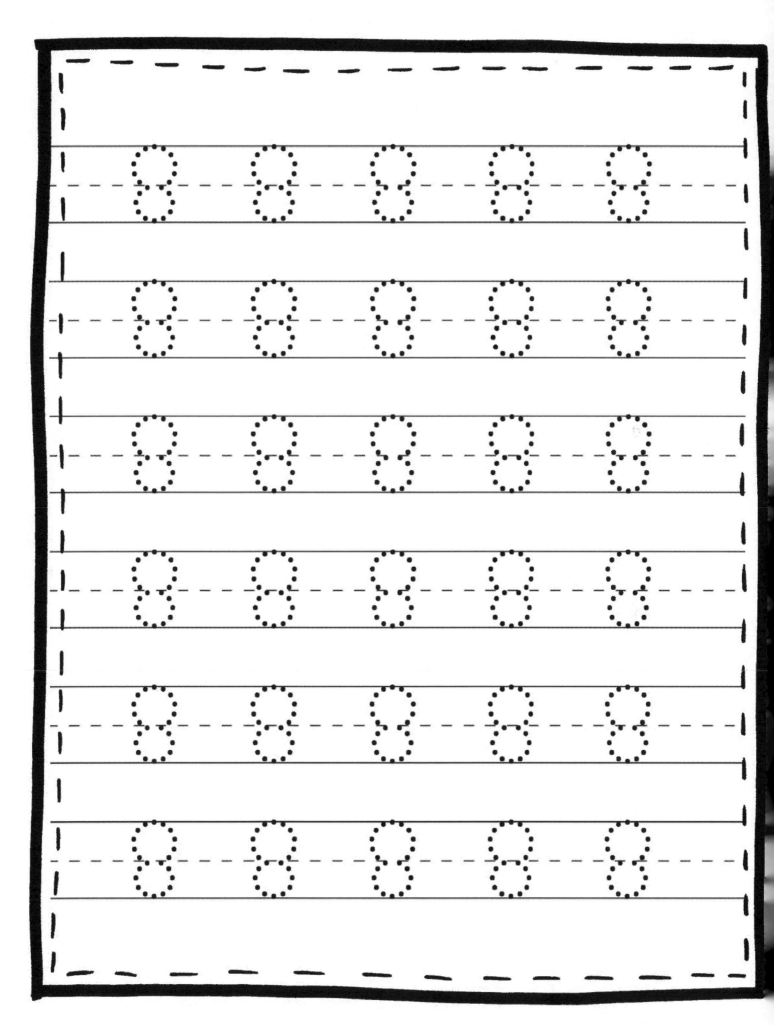

Trace and write the number.

9 9 9 9 9 9 9 9 9

Color the number word.

nine

Show the number on the ten frame.

Color 9 stars.

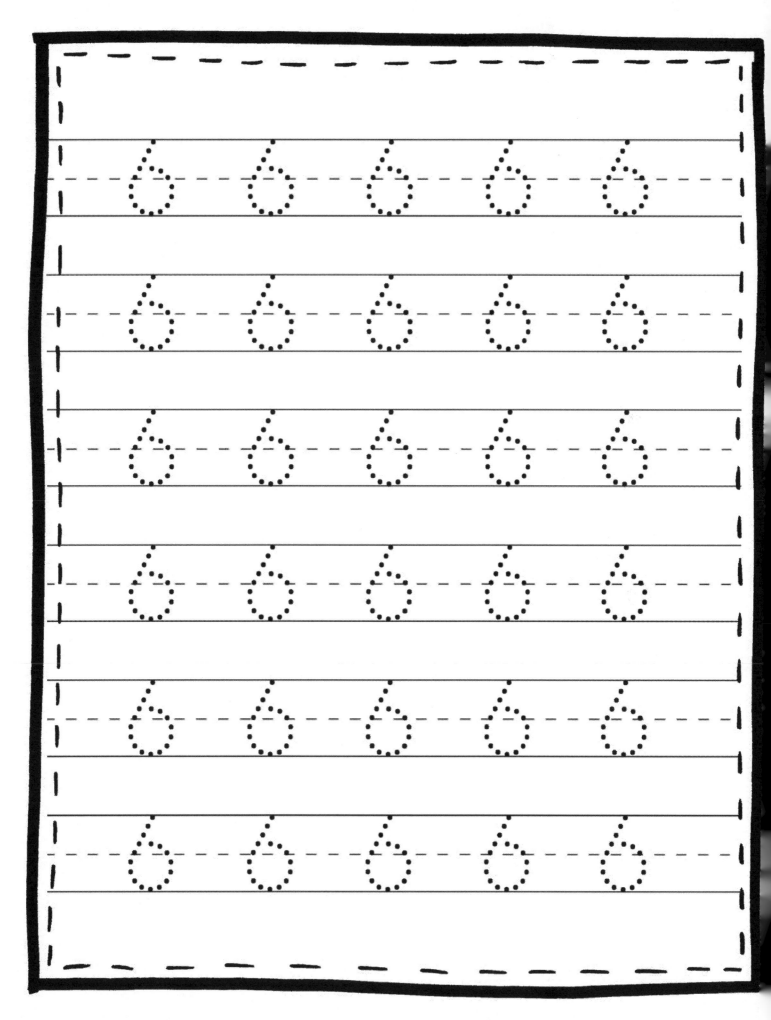

Color 10 stars.

Show the number on the ten frame.

ten

Color the number word.

Trace and write the number.

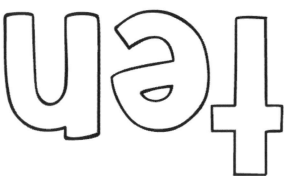

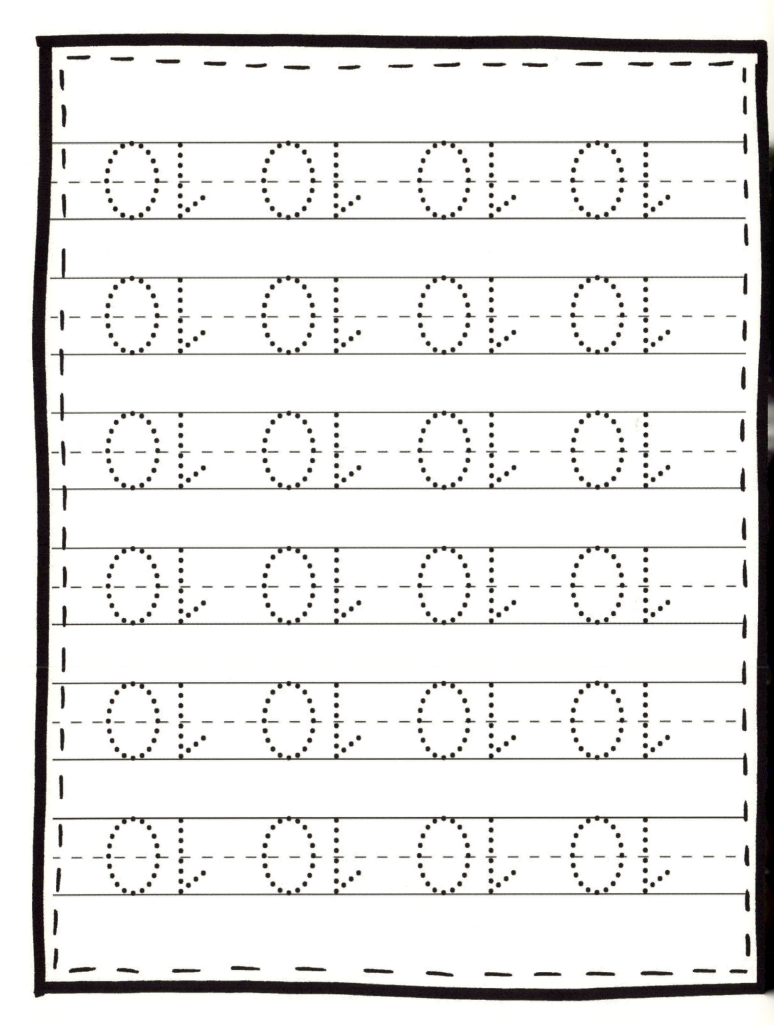

Made in the USA
Middletown, DE
27 January 2019